BRITAIN IN OLD PHOTOGRAPHS

HALESOWEN

DAVID L. EADES

SUTTON PUBLISHING LIMITED

Sutton Publishing Limited
Phoenix Mill · Thrupp · Stroud
Gloucestershire · GL5 2BU

First published 1998

Reprinted with corrections 1999

Title page photograph:
St John the Baptist's church, Halesowen, 1928.
Some twelfth-century fragments still remain but
most of the structure dates from the fourteenth
and fifteenth centuries. The tower collapsed
during the fifteenth century, and its
replacement is unusually positioned in the
middle of the nave. Among the many
interesting features in the church are a large Norman
font and the coffin of a fourteenth-century priest.

British Library Cataloguing in Publication Data
A catalogue record for this book is available from the
British Library.

ISBN 0-7509-2032-7

Typeset in 10/12 Perpetua.
Typesetting and origination by
Sutton Publishing Limited
Printed in GreatBritain by
Ebenezer Baylis, Worcester

THE BLACK COUNTRY SOCIETY

This voluntary society, affiliated to the Civic Trust, was founded in 1967 as a reaction to the trend of the late 1950s and early 1960s to amalgamate everything into large units and in the Midlands to sweep away the area's industrial heritage in the process.

The general aim of the Society is to create interest in the past, present and future of the Black Country, and early on it campaigned for the establishment of an industrial museum. In 1975 the Black Country Living Museum was started by Dudley Borough Council on 26 acres of totally derelict land adjoining the grounds of Dudley Castle. This has developed into an award-winning museum which attracts over 250,000 visitors annually.

It was announced in August 1998 that having secured a lottery grant of nearly £3 million, the Museum Board will be able to authorize the start of work on a £4.5 million state-of-the-art interpretation centre. This will be known as the 'Rolfe Street Project', named after the street which once housed the Smethwick Baths. The façade of this Victorian building is to be incorporated into the new interpretation centre.

At the Black Country Living Museum there is a boat dock fully equipped to restore narrowboats of wood and iron and different vessels can be seen on the dock throughout the year. From behind the Bottle and Glass Inn visitors can travel on a canal boat into Dudley Canal Tunnel, a memorable journey to see spectacular limestone caverns and the fascinating Castle Mill Basin.

There are 2,500 members of the Black Country Society and all receive the quarterly magazine *The Blackcountryman*, of which 124 issues have been published since its founding in 1967. In the whole collection there are some 1,800 authoritative articles on all aspects of the Black Country by historians, teachers, researchers, students, subject experts and ordinary folk with an extraordinary story to tell. The whole constitutes a unique resource about the area and is a mine of information for students and researchers who frequently refer to it. Many schools and libraries are subscribers. Three thousand copies of the magazine are printed each quarter. It is non-commercial, and contributors do not receive payment for their articles.

PO Box 71 · Kingswinford · West Midlands DY6 9YN

CONTENTS

Halesowen town centre, *c.* 1750.

INTRODUCTION

The map of Halesowen town centre opposite is mainly conjecture, and shows the town in about 1750. The road junction to the north of the church was always known to the natives as the Townsend. Newcomers to Halesowen, or those born in the last thirty years, know the junction – now an island and a very busy thoroughfare – as the Earlsway Island, a name derived from the Earls Brook, a tributary of the River Stour that runs very near. A comparison of this map with the one reproduced in the Halesowen Borough Official Guide Book of 1949 would show that although there had been many changes they had not transformed the area, and there were still many wide open spaces. A similar comparison with a present-day map would see many more roads, and far less open space. So things do not stand still.

The object of this book is not to present a full history, but to create a record of a town which has greatly changed, and to recapture some of the places and the people which have made the once lovely old town of Halesowen tick. The places covered by the book have been roughly confined to the area which once formed the municipal borough of Halesowen, 1936–74. Very little has been included of Cradley because three publications on that township in recent years have served the area well. However, it is good to remember that the Rural District of Halesowen covered, in addition to the town, the areas of Hill and Cakemore, Cradley, Hasbury and Lutley, Hawne, Lapal and Illey, Quinton, Lye and Wollescote. Lye and Wollescote was formed into an urban district in 1897, and Quinton joined the City Of Birmingham in 1909. Halesowen was formed into an urban district in 1925, and the town celebrated obtaining borough status in 1936, being one of the few boroughs created during the brief reign of King Edward VIII, later the Duke of Windsor. Let it not be forgotten, though, that Halesowen was a borough in the Middle Ages. Its first charter was gained in 1270, achieved really at the behest of Halesowen Abbey. This proved to be a mixed blessing, and it was not until the townsfolk managed to rid themselves of feudal dues to the Abbey that they were able to benefit from their new found 'freedom'. The Dissolution of Halesowen Abbey took place in 1538.

The town of Halesowen lies in a hollow, hence the first part of the name 'Hala' from the Old English (Anglo Saxon) – meaning recess, secret place, something hidden away. It is often used to mean a small hollow in the slope of a hillside. In 1177 Henry II granted the Manor of Hales to his brother-in-law, David ap Owen. So there is very little doubt that the suffix Owen was taken from the Welsh prince, and was used as a means of distinguishing the manor from Hailes Abbey in Gloucestershire and other villages of that name.

The Domesday Book entry for Halesowen after the Norman Conquest in 1066 confirms its traditional position as part of Worcestershire: 'In Clent Hundred Earl Roger, holds of the King, 1 Manor called Halas.' The Earl Roger of this entry is our local link with national events. The famous Roger de Montgomery had led the right wing of the Norman forces at the Battle of Hastings, and for this service to his Duke had been created Earl of Shrewsbury, made over-lord of that county and Montgomeryshire and had been given the Manor of Halas. Promptly Roger unified his possessions by causing the Manor of Halas to be detached from Worcestershire and annexed to Shropshire, where it stayed until 1844.

A Shropshire guide of 1829 describes Halesowen thus:

Hales Owen, a borough town, situated in an insulated parish of the same name, separated from the county of Shropshire, and entirely surrounded by Staffordshire and Worcestershire, the town and borough extending into the hundred of Halfshire, in the latter county . . . Lord Lyttleton is the Lord of the manor, who holds an annual court Leet, when a high and low bailiff, a constable and a headborough are appointed; a court for the recovery of debts under 40s. is also holden every three weeks at the Lyttleton's Arms Inn. This place has been noted for the manufactory of nails, and pearl and horn buttons; there is also an extensive concern under the firm of "The British Iron Company" at Corngreaves; and some new coal mines are now opening in the parish. The River Stour, which rises in some hills not far distant, runs through the borough, and the Netherton canal passes about half a mile from the town. The parish church contains a beautiful monument to the memory of Major Halliday, and a plain one to Shenstone the poet. The benefice is a vicarage, in the patronage of Lord Lyttelton, and incumbency of the Revd G. Biggs. Here are also a chapel each for the Independent and Wesleyan Methodists; and a free school for the education of boys in the classics. About half a mile from the town are the ruins of the Manor Abbey founded in the reign of King John; part of the walls are yet standing, but overgrown with bushes and weeds. A short distance from the town are the Leasowes, the seat of the immortal Shenstone; and three miles south-east from this place, at Frankley, there was formerly a seat of that profound lawyer Sir Thomas Lyttelton, the celebrated lawyer of the 'Tenures' whose descendant was George; created Baron of Frankley and Lord Lyttelton in 1757. This seat having been burnt down by Prince Rupert in the civil wars, and never rebuilt; the family removed to Hagley. The country round here is fertile; its general appearance pleasing and agricultural, presenting an agreeable admixture of hill and dale. There are two fairs held in the year; viz the first on Easter Monday and the other on 22nd June. The parish of Hales Owen is ten miles in length and seven in breadth, and that part of it situated in the county of Shropshire contained in 1821 81,867 inhabitants, while those in the town and borough amounted to 1,759; total in the entire parish, 10,946.

We trust that through this book there will be found a flavour of the foregoing as the pictures unfold of this ancient and much-loved town. And furthermore, we hope that if you have old photographs hidden away you may be willing to lend them, so that more of Halesowen's past can be preserved for future generations to enjoy – contact the author through the publishers!

The armorial bearings of the Borough of Halesowen (reproduced by kind permission of Dudley Metropolitan Borough Council). The crest shows a mural crown, and arising therefrom an anvil, symbolic of the iron and steel industry of the district, with a gold chain in allusion to the chain industry of Cradley. The shield displays an appropriate arrangement of the emblems taken from the arms of the principal owners of the Manor of Hales: Earl Roger de Montgomery (who held the Manor of Hales 1066–94) – that portion of the lion rampant coloured red; Robert Dudley, Earl of Leicester (1555) – that portion of the lion rampant coloured green on a gold ground; the Premonstratensian Canons of Halesowen (1218–1538) – the fleur-de-lys on blue ground; and Viscount Cobham, representing the Lyttelton family (since 1559) – the two escallops. The supporters: on the left side is a canon of the Premonstratensian Order to represent the Abbot of Halesowen Abbey, and that on the right is a gentleman of the early fifteenth century to represent Sir Thomas Lyttelton, Lord Chief Justice of the Court of Common Pleas. The motto 'Respice, Aspice, Prospice' may be read: 'Look to the past, the present and the future'.

CHAPTER ONE

SCENES

High Street, c. 1963. The turreted building is the old post office and the archway led to the post office yard. It will be observed that the buildings between the post office and the church have already been demolished to make way for the Queensway. In the other direction Wrenson's the grocers still remained, though now long since gone, and Halesowen's first supermarket Fine Fare – now occupied by Wilkinson's – was already open. (Phil Waldren)

Official opening of Halesowen's first purpose-built supermarket in High Street, *c.* 1963. The Dagenham Girl Pipers led the celebrations, and during the first week eight thousand chickens were given away: one was given to each customer who spent a set amount (possibly £2). (*Michael Dancer*)

A view up High Street, *c.* 1960. The Lyttleton Arms is on the right. It was commonly called Billy Pick's because William Pick was the licensee from before 1932 to 1942, and it was in the Pick family until 1957. Some of the old buildings remain. Shops on this side of the road housed Cash Clothing, Heague's newsagents, Sturman's Sadlers, Hilton's shoe shop, Tenant's chemists, Ebourne's fruiterer, Peplow's jewellers and A. & D. Wimbush & Son (formerly Major Hackett's shop). Heague's was a newsagents and confectioners, and sold gelatine lozenges for 3*d*.

Hagley Street *c.* 1950. This view is taken from Great Cornbow and shows the old shops adjacent to Lloyd's Bank. The bank remains but modern buildings housing Iceland and the Britannia Building Society replace the shops. The blinds are down over Charlie Peach's grocery shop, and to its right is H. Parkes, printers. On the immediate right of the picture are the railings of the old Congregational chapel, where the Midland Bank now stands. (*Margaret Westwood*)

High Street from Church Street with the church wall on the right and the old market cross, *c.* 1955. The first block of buildings on the right was demolished to allow the road to swing right to form Queensway. The first three buildings housed Grove's solicitors (Church Steps), Dickie Willets, fruiterer and Roper's. Roper's was a hat shop, and many will remember Mrs Roper, who used to say 'Come forward please'. Further down into the town can be seen the sign outside Ye Olde Lyttleton Arms, the upstairs bay windows of W.S. Welch & Son (haberdasher), and, to the left in the centre of the town, the old Congregational chapel, which had not yet been demolished. (*Phil Waldren*)

Church Lane, formerly known as Dog Lane, c. 1955. The black and white cottages on the left are now one house, known as Whitefriars. The building on the right, where the car park is now situated, was formerly the Malt Shovel public house. In latter years it was the home of the Bailey family, who ran the adjacent fish and chip shop in Church Street. (*Phil Waldren*)

Entrance to Church Street, 1950s. It was for one way traffic only and seems no wider today than it did then. The parish church gates are on the left with the old market cross. Dearne and Raistrick occupied the first shop on the right, with the HMV sign. Leopard's Yard was in between this shop and the next large building, which was the Old Rectory; this had been enlarged to take Archdeacon Hone's big family. The last rector to live there was Canon Colville, who moved to Highfields House. In the 1920s and '30s the young people of the parish church played tennis in the grounds of the Rectory and attended handicraft classes there. It ended its days converted into flatlets. The next building along, with windows in the roof, was where Halesowen folk went to have 'tatch and end', Black Country dialect for having shoes repaired with a waxed thread at Wade's. (*Phil Waldren*)

Church Street – renamed High Street now, late 1950s or early '60s. The photograph shows buildings from the top of Church Lane along to Ivy House, which still remains, but the other buildings were demolished to make way for the concrete car park opposite the parish church. The first building at the top of Church Lane was the Malt Shovel. Other shops along that row were Bailey's fish and chip shop, Mrs Southall's sweet shop (Mrs Southall wore glasses on the end of her nose, and you had to go down a step to enter the shop) and Harrison's electrical and gown shops. The two post ladies, Mrs Shilvock and Mrs Barton, occupied the house with the bay windows immediately next to Ivy House. Their curtains were crocheted. (*Phil Waldren*)

Rosa's sweet shop in Peckingham Street, 1950s. Mr Johnny Rosa had been an Italian soldier and was interned during the Second World War. The shop was situated opposite Dancer's at the bottom end of Peckingham Street. Many children will recall, as does the author, consuming beautiful Italian ice cream from glass dishes in this shop. Johnny Rosa used to sell ice cream from a side box attached to his BSA motorbike which he rode around the locality. The side box was filled with ice, and ice cream of course!

Williams' fishmongers in Peckingham Street, *c*. 1900. Mrs Williams always wore her straw hat and white apron, and invariably there was a white cat sitting in the window. The young man in the picture is Joseph Reuben Parsons, a member of the family. Joseph's sister Polly became a nun.

Dancers store on the corner of Peckingham Street, prior to demolition and the building of more modern premises. This photograph was taken by Mr Michael Dancer on 12 March 1967, and shows his grandparents, Mr and Mrs Wilfred Dancer, looking on. The business was in the throes of moving to its temporary home in the old Co-op department at the top of Peckingham Street. Next to Dancers was Dick Marsh's meat shop.

Hagley Street, late 1950s. This shows the town centre before redevelopment. Dancers old store is on the left, and the only building remaining today on the right is Lloyd's Bank. This picture was obviously taken on a very quiet Sunday morning, because this road was not pedestrianised as it is now, but was a busy thoroughfare. The shops were occupied by George Bridge butchers, Mary Moseley's clothes shop, Lloyd's Bank, Peach's grocery store, H. Parkes Ltd, printers, Charlie Grainger's fruit shop, J. Taylor's shoes, Hawkeswood's haberdasher, alley to Beasleys Garage, Pagett's ironmongers – taken over by Willetts' fruit store, Valeting Service, Marsh and Baxter's Meats, passage way to the old market hall – and just in the picture on the extreme right is George Mason's, grocers. (*Phil Waldren*)

Peckingham Street prior to redevelopment, *c.* 1960. The shop at the top, opposite Maison Hetty's, was occupied by Hollies, butchers. Next to the shop was Hollies House. The gable-ended building used to be a pub called the Globe. The two shops on the extreme right of the picture were occupied by Bannister's shoe repairers and Timmins' newsagents.

Great Cornbow, *c.* 1955, opposite the Council House, showing Knight's, wallpaper shop and their house. The shop below Knight's was occupied by J. Henn, chartered accountants. The Congregational chapel was round the corner in Hagley Street. The whole of this site is now occupied by the Midland Bank. (*Phil Waldren*)

Bull Ring, directly opposite the Council House, late 1950s. Next to Hollies, the butchers at the top of Peckingham Street, on the extreme right of the photograph, is the old Crown, renamed Crown Chambers by the solicitor, A.G. Rudge, who purchased the pub for use as his offices. (*Phil Waldren*)

The rear of the Co-op premises in Birmingham Street, *c.* 1960. (*Phil Waldren*)

Looking down Peckingham Street, *c.* 1963. The building on the extreme left of the photograph is the old Bethel Mission. Some new buildings are in place: Fine Fare supermarket, Foster Brothers and Woolworths. The old buildings on the right here were the Co-op coal and food offices, and on the corner with Birmingham Street was the Co-op drapery shop; the manageress was Miss Minnie Partridge. (*Phil Waldren*)

Houses along Richmond Street, *c.* 1960. On the far right of the picture can be seen the junction with Islington. (*Phil Waldren*)

Richmond Street at its junction with Hales Road, *c.* 1955. The old school sign, the torch of learning, alerts motorists to the Church School entrance half way down Hales Road, or Cemetery Lane as it used to be named – and is still so called by older Halesowen residents.

Hill Street before redevelopment, *c.* 1955. Ansells outdoor licence, the Golden Cup, was kept by the Shilvock family. The Williams' family lived next door but one. Does any one recognise the lady with the mop? In 1906 the Halesowen Justices resolved 'That in the opinion of the Justices . . . there are too many licences in proportion to the population, and that steps be taken under the Licensing Act of 1904 to reduce them', and it was further resolved at a later meeting that the Star and Garter Inn, Birmingham Street, Leopard Inn, Church Street, and The Golden Cross Inn, Peckingham Street, were not needed. The lady on the step is Lily Partridge. (*Phil Waldren*)

New Street, *c.* 1955. The building on the extreme left is the British Arms Inn. This street disappeared with the redevelopment of the town. It was parallel to the Hagley Road, behind the Nelson Public House, and also parallel with Hill Street. (*Phil Waldren*)

Houses in Gaunts Yard, *c.* 1955. (*Michael Dancer*)

Houses at the top of Islington, *c.* 1955. (*Phil Waldren*)

Rear of houses in Gaunts Yard, *c.* 1955. The wall of the churchyard and trees on the left are all that remains of this scene today, and the buildings have been replaced by the limited time parking bays opposite the post office. The building to the left is the Old Rectory in Church Street. (*Phil Waldren*)

Demolition of old buildings in Gaunts Yard near the parish church, as roads are laid in Highfields Park in preparation for the redevelopment of the town centre, *c.* 1960. (*Phil Waldren*)

Hagley Street, 1970s, when redevelopment was as we thought completed – but, alas, further vandalism was to take place with the demolition of the old public library and Council Chamber, to be replaced by the Cornbow Hall and shops. (*Wesley Dancer*)

Houses in Birmingham Road, *c.* 1960. The large old premises on the left are where David Aupret, veterinary surgeon, used to practise. Behind these buildings can be seen new premises erected in Peckingham Street. (*Phil Waldren*)

Bundle Hill, *c.* 1955 – so named because of its proximity to the residences of many of the poorest nailers, who used to carry their bundles of nails up it. At the entrance to Bundle Hill can be observed the gables of Bundle Hill House where Dr C.A. Mather and Dr A.N. Fotheringham, general practitioners, used to have their surgery. Further up the hill is the entrance to Otterbourne Court, the home of the Homfray family, and later Frank Somers. Otterbourne Court is now the headquarters of the Halesowen British Legion. In the distance, behind the wooden pole, can be seen the Halesowen gasometer in Great Cornbow, and further in the distance are the fields of Webbs Green Farm, where the Abbeyfields Estate was built. (*Phil Waldren*)

Halesowen station platform and ticket office, *c.* 1960. The station was situated on the left as one begins to ascend Mucklow Hill, just below Prospect Road. The lines from Dudley to Old Hill, with an intermediate station at Windmill End, and from Old Hill to Halesowen were formally opened on 1 March 1878. The event was not marked with any public ceremony, but a celebration luncheon was held at the New Inn, Halesowen, with the Hon. C.J. Lyttleton in the chair. Mr H.W. Payton was the stationmaster during the early years of this century, and the station was noted for its beautiful flowerbeds. (*Peter Barnsley*)

Signal-box at Halesowen station, *c.* 1969, when the demolition of the station had commenced. The signal-box was adjacent to the platform on the opposite side of the line to the ticket offices. The station closed completely on 9 September 1968, and this picture shows the commencement of the demolition of the station buildings and the taking up of the track. This was a sad day for Halesowen because a station would be of untold benefit to the town today. (*Peter Barnsley*)

Hayley Green Isolation Hospital, where infectious diseases were treated, *c.* 1900. Three wards were named after early members of the Joint Hospital Board: Waugh, Hodgetts and Parkes. Pavilion Ward was where patients suffering from tuberculosis were treated. It was at the rear of the hospital grounds and faced Clent: the wards and the wooden cubicles were designed to be open to the fresh air, the only known treatment for TB. This photograph shows the main entrance to the hospital on the Hagley Road, with Waugh Ward on the left and the main hospital administration block and kitchens on the right. The gates were widened in the 1960s. Eventually the wall was demolished and rebuilt when the site was developed after the closure of the hospital in 1996.

The main administrative block, which, in the early days of the hospital, also served as a nurses' home. Today it is private apartments.

Hayley Green Isolation Hospital, *c.* 1900. Patients and nurses take the air on the lawn in front of Waugh Ward with the main block to the left.

Hayley Green Isolation Hospital, *c.* 1900. This is the inside of one of the wards, possibly Waugh Ward.

The Small Pox Hospital, Lutley, which lay down a track off Grove's Lane. The hospital was situated behind where Halesowen fire station is now, roughly in the Hazeldene Road area. The hospital was inhabited in the 1930s by Mr and Mrs Gaunt and their three children, Michael, John and Janet. Janet married Mr Tom Hardwicke of Quarry Lane, and he purchased the hospital in the 1940s. It was demolished in the late 1950s. (*Stourbridge Library*)

Bloomfield Street, *c.* 1920. Apart from the demolition of the building on the extreme right of the picture, and the erec of a modern house this year (1998) where the fence is, nothing much has altered.

Hagley Road *c.* 1970. The mix of old and new buildings house (from left) the MEB showroom, Broome's greengrocery shop and Fereday and Cooke, a TV and radio shop. Townsfolk used to walk down the side of the MEB showroom to reach Halesowen Fairground. These buildings were situated where the island is opposite the United Church, at the junction with Queensway.

Hagley Road, 1980. Redevelopment is complete. The white building straight ahead is the Husky Dog, now rebuilt and used as solicitors' offices.

Shenstone Inn, at the corner of Bromsgrove Street and Birmingham Road, now Whitehall Road, 1960s. The junction with Mucklow Hill, Dudley Road and Bromsgrove Street was a crossroads controlled by traffic lights. The Shenstone Inn was on the opposite corner of Bromsgrove Street as you approached down Mucklow Hill. (*Peter Barnsley*)

Mucklow Hill, late 1960s – when it was still a single carriageway. The buildings on the right, beyond the trees, belong to the Halesowen Steel Company. The building at the end of this row – Vulcan Works – still remains. (*Peter Barnsley*)

Birmingham Road at the foot of Mucklow Hill, *c.* 1970. Demolition of the Shenstone Inn is in progress. The large building to the right is the former Shenstone Methodist church. (*Peter Barnsley*)

Demolition of Shenstone Inn and adjacent buildings, from Dudley Road, *c.* 1970. (*Peter Barnsley*)

Opening of the new Co-op drapery store in Hagley Street, next to Lloyd's Bank, *c.* 1965. The photograph was taken from behind the railings where the Congregational chapel had once stood, now the Midland Bank. Iceland now occupies the Co-op's premises. (*Michael Dancer*)

Hagley Street from the opposite end, and a little earlier than the photograph above. The Chocolate Box Café on the left had already been demolished. The next group of buildings, occupied by Chapman's opticians and Bridge the butchers, were already reserved. The new Co-op building is being built but the other older buildings in that row were still standing.

The Liberal Club on the corner of Hagley Street and Laurel Lane, 23 April 1957. The buildings are decorated for the visit of Her Majesty the Queen and the Duke of Edinburgh on that day. The large building to the left is the Council House garage, which was situated behind the public library and Council Chamber building. (*Margaret Westwood*)

Belle Vue at the top of Mucklow Hill. The property had once been the home of Edward Gem, and at the time it was bought by Walter Somers in 1907 it was owned by the Homfray family. Walter Somers paid £2,250 for the property. The building became the headquarters of the MEB and was much extended. At the end of 1998 new owners will take over and the building will commence a new chapter in its history.

Side view of Highfields House, *c.* 1955. The house was formerly situated in what remains today of Highfields Park – to the side of Walton Campus, Bundle Hill. The house was eventually converted into flats in the 1950s. (*Phil Waldren*)

Front elevation of Highfields House, *c.* 1920s. The Revd G. Burr is standing to the right of the front door. The bandstand in Highfields Park was eventually converted into the Sons of Rest Club; when it was demolished a wing of Highfields House was retained (the remainder having been demolished) for the Sons of Rest to use. The Burr family owned Lutley Mill, and when they moved to Highfields they took the clock from Lutley and had it placed above the coach house.

Huntingtree House, now the Huntingtree public house in Alexandra Road, *c.* 1920. The house was formerly the home of the Grove family who owned the Grove button factory. It was agreed by the Justices in 1947 that the licence should be provisionally moved from the New Inns to a site at Huntingtree. A final order was made on 1 November 1955.

Quinton Farm, Hagley Road West, *c.* 1930. This building, the site of which is now occupied by the King's Highway Hotel, was also known as Tinker's Farm, Quintain Green or Moncton House, and was rebuilt in 1750. It was the home of Ambrose Foley, a feoffee of Halesowen Free School, who entertained John Wesley and was responsible for inviting him to come to Quinton.

The Grange, *c*. 1900, now the Sports and Social Club near to the island at the foot of Grange Hill. The house was the home of the Lea-Smith family and was built by Ferdinando Dudley Lea-Smith in about 1750, though there had been a dwelling of sorts on the site since the abbey had been built in 1218. The last member of the Lea-Smith family to live in the house (see page 111) was responsible for reviving the title of Lord Dudley, and his daughter, the Baroness Dudley, still lives in Worcestershire. Various tenants occupied the house and grounds in succeeding years and it is not certain when it was eventually sold. During the First World War part of the house was used as a military hospital, and during the Second World War Italian prisoners of war were housed there. Seth Somers and his family lived at The Grange for a time before they moved to Bell Hall, Belbroughton. The house and immediate grounds form the Sports and Social Club, while the larger grounds, including the Halesowen cricket ground, form the Seth Somers Park which is owned by the Seth Somers Trust. At one time, before the Halesowen by-pass was built, the grounds extended from the top of Grange Hill into Dog Kennel Lane, where there were the Grange Mill and orchards owned by the Lea-Smiths and beyond Waxland Road.

Grange Road, roughly from the intersection of the roads opposite the Woodman, c. 1927. The building at the end of the road is the Vine Inn, and that stretch of road is still called Vine Lane today. The gasometer is to the right, and the high grassy bank is occupied by houses now; behind them is McDonald's.

Grange Hill, c. 1920. Gone are the days when a cyclist who had an accident outside Mrs Talbot's house could be left quite safely in the road while she went to telephone for help.

Birch Hill waterfalls, *c.* 1909. These falls were situated off Mucklow Hill, and when the road was made into a dual carriageway the water was culverted under the road.

The redeveloped town centre, *c.* 1970. In the distance are the gasometer and the Co-op Model Dairy – replaced now by McDonald's. In the foreground of the photograph is the car park on which Maybrook House was built. To the centre right is the open-air precinct, now covered in and re-named the Cornbow Centre.

Wartime water tank in Springfield Road, Hill and Cakemore, 1968. This tank housed water in case of fire; the fire engine emptied it before its demolition. Houses now occupy the site. In the background of the lower picture is Dudley and Dowells Foundry, eventually demolished.

Boats on the canal near Mucklow Hill, *c.* 1960. Trips could be taken to the Black Horse Pub, Manor Lane, now Manor Way, and up to the entrance of the Lapal Tunnel. Boats were also available on the Lady Pool at the Leasowes. The pool was so named because for a few years around 1900 the Anstey Physical Training College started its life at the Leasowes under the autocratic leadership of Miss Anstey. Physical fitness was the order of the day, with the girls swimming in Shenstone's icy pools – hence the Lady Pool! (*Phil Waldren*)

Fishing in the countryside: Foredrove Bridge on Green's Farm, *c.* 1960. Abbeyfields Estate was built on Green's Farm, off Manor Lane, Halesowen. The parish church can be seen in the distance. (*Phil Waldren*)

Stone cottages in Hasbury, Wall Well, *c.* 1930. These cottages faced the present Hasbury Methodist church, and the gate to the left led to High Farm. The Farley family lived in the double-fronted cottage. They were all demolished in 1934.

Back Lane Hasbury (now Albert Road), *c.* 1930. The barn on the left belonged to High Farm.

Old Barn Farm, Hasbury, directly opposite the old Hasbury chapel in Wall Well, 1930. To the left of the two-storey barn in the upper picture can be seen the Hasbury chapel schoolroom, and behind the barn in the lower picture can be seen the gable end of the old Hasbury chapel, built in 1860 and demolished in 1971. Mr Arthur Timmins, a local builder and undertaker, purchased these barns and behind them he built The Summit, for occupation by himself and his family. Additions were made to the barns, and they were made into the Old Barn House and Wall Well House in 1920. These properties were demolished in 1969. The Summit still stands, but in its once large grounds the road Summit Gardens has been formed and houses have been built. (*Mrs Margaret Roberts, Arthur Timmins' daughter*)

Interior of the infirmary of Halesowen Abbey.
The watercolour was painted by Halesowen
artist Lyndon G. Harris in about 1945.

Halesowen Abbey: a watercolour by Lyndon G. Harris, *c.* 1944.

Harvesting scene, Halesowen Abbey Barn: an oil painting by Lyndon G. Harris, *c.* 1949. The barn is situated roughly on the site of the abbey's northern cloister.

Washing day under the walls of Halesowen Abbey, painted by Lyndon G. Harris in 1947. This oil painting was entered for the Slade School Summer Composition Competition, when it was awarded an honourable mention. It was subsequently exhibited at several exhibitions, including the Paris Salon where it was awarded a Mention Honourable.

An aquatint of Halesowen Parish Church and the buildings in Birmingham Street from the gas works by Lyndon G. Harris. It is based on a watercolour by the same artist of about 1946.

Halesowen church from Highfields by Charles Leaver, 1877. The artist flourished from 1867 to 1883. He was a painter of landscapes and rural subjects, and he specialised in atmospheric 'church in snow' pictures in which he framed the parish church in frosty scenes. Leaver was based in Harborne and frequently exhibited at the Royal Birmingham Society of Artists. He travelled a great deal around Britain.

'Halesowen, Shropshire', drawn and engraved by J. Storer for *The Beauties of England and Wales*.

Halesowen, *c.* 1802, engraved by J. Greig from a drawing by M.D. Parkes.

The parish church and Church Street, usually called The Townsend, *c*. 1900. The black and white cottages on the right at the entrance to the Church Schools were demolished in the 1950s. Halesowen Borough Council considered making them into a museum but it was not possible because of the cost. The public house on the extreme right of the photograph, the George, still remains.

Hagley Road, 1920. The buildings on the left still remain, though the frontages have changed somewhat. The shop on the left was Parish's Pianos, and next door to him was Mr Morris, the pawnbroker. Modern edifices replace the buildings on the right. Today just beyond the trees is an island and a busy intersection with Queensway.

A rural idyll in Halesowen: Cemetery Avenue, *c.* 1900.

Demolition of old buildings in Rumbow, 1960s. The double-fronted house used to be a seed shop. (*Michael Dancer*)

, charabanc trip (possibly a works outing) leaving H. Parkes Ltd, Hagley Street, 1920s. Harry Parkes is standing to the ight with his eldest son Wilf on his left. Will Parkes, the brother of Harry, is sitting towards the front of the vehicle vearing a trilby. Miss Beatrice Maiden, who worked in the bindery department, is sitting in the centre, and standing at ie rear are Jim Taylor and Frank Jones. Howard Taylor, who later founded Reliance Printing, is seated, wearing a dark iirt.

Hagley Street, 1960s. New buildings are under construction next to H. Parkes Ltd. There do not appear to be any shoes on display in Taylor's window, so they must have already moved to the Queensway near to the post office. H. Parkes appear to be having their closing down sale. (*Michael Dancer*)

Dancers shop on the corner of Hagley Street and Peckingham Street, *c*. 1890. Beyond the shops can be observed the St
of David on the gable of the Congregational chapel. It is thought that the advertising board above the light-walled buildin
was originally placed there as a screen for magic lantern shows, which were projected from the buildings opposite on th
occasion of Queen Victoria's Diamond Jubilee in 1897. Another story says that a great sheet was fixed to th
Congregational chapel railings.

The old market cross, Great Cornbow, 1900. The cross now stands in the churchyard. It marked the town's market and fair, and may have come originally from Halesowen Abbey. It was once possibly more ornate, but religious symbols may have been removed during the Reformation. After a gale on 22 February 1908, during which the cross blew down, it was dumped on a rubbish tip. A local solicitor and clerk to the Justices Mr Alfred Homfray rescued it, and Mr Job Garratt, the owner of New Hawne Colliery, paid for its recovery and re-erection in the churchyard.

Mr Job Garratt, local businessman and Justice of the Peace. He lived at Wassell Grove.

Halesowen parish church, from behind buildings in High Street, 1960. (*Phil Waldren*)

CHAPTER TWO

CHAPELS & CHURCHES

A stained glass memorial window at Short Cross Methodist church. The window was given to the church by Mr and Mrs Joseph Parsons and family in memory of the scholars of the Church and Sunday School who had died during the First World War. Messrs H. Hope & Sons of Smethwick executed the work, and it was dedicated on 26 February 1928. It was originally in the old church at Short Cross, and when the new church was built in 1934 the window was repositioned. The brass memorial plaque attached to the window is inscribed: 'To The Glory of God and In Memory Of George Eden, Thomas Eden, Thomas W. Lee, Leonard Sawyer, Percy Smith, Harry Williams Who Fell In The Great War 1914–1918.'

The window represents the sorrow of mankind and the hope of the Resurrection. 'The six motifs in the side panels express the Anchor of Hope, the Mirror and Lamp of Truth and Light, the Book and Scroll of Knowledge and the Tree of Life. The Air Force, Army and Navy are represented at the bottom by the Eagle, Helmet, Rifle, Sword and the Anchor respectively. The bowed figure of Victory, with the wreath laid on the flowers – emblems of eternal life – suggests the grief and tragedy of war. The Olive Tree – symbol of peace – is rising from the weapons of strife – the shield, sword and helmet. Continuing the original idea is the ascending figure of Christ, showing the triumph of Life over Death. The hands are extended in benediction, giving the assurance that the souls of the righteous are in the hands of God.'

Zion Methodist Church, Stourbridge Road, 1966. This building was built by a band of Methodist New Connexion stalwarts who had already started meeting for worship in their old chapel in 1825 in Brook Road, off Birmingham Street. During the ministry of the Revd W. Seaton it was decided to build a new chapel, so 348 square yards of land at 3s per yard, namely £52 4s, were purchased from Lord Lyttleton on 20 December 1841, the stonelaying ceremony was held on Monday 13 June, and the chapel was opened for public worship on 4 December 1842. The building ceased to be used as a Methodist church in 1979 and was sold to Emery Estates Ltd. The proceeds of the sale, approximately £17,000, were used to help defray the expenses in 1985 of the extensions to Hasbury Methodist church, which cost £55,000. In 1981 the Zion Pentecostal church began meeting there for worship. The building is now converted into offices and is called Church Court. In 1854 John Noake wrote: 'The Zion Chapel rears its plain but untasteful proportions.' In 1976 the chapel was listed as being of special architectural and historical interest!

The old Methodist New Connexion chapel, Brook Road, Birmingham Street, c. 1966. After the building ceased to be used as a church, it was used as a fruit store for Grainger's, the fruiterers. (*Michael Dancer*)

Congregational chapel, Hagley Street, *c.* 1900. The church was opened for public worship in 1811. In 1809 Joseph Harris and Samuel Whall on behalf of the church bought the site which was an open space where poplar trees grew, and belonged to Walter Woodcok, for £126. The early adherents agreed to form themselves into a church on 15 September 1907. The first seven members of the congregation were George Taylor, Thomas Golden, Joseph Harris, Thomas Hunt, Benjamin Hodkins, Benjamin Brettell and John Sawyer. The first women members were Alice Hodgkins, Mary Cole, Ann Hunt, Sarah Hodgkins, Mary Hodgkins, Phoebe Parish and Ann Rice.

Congregational church interior, Hagley Street, *c.* 1900. The church has a history going back to 1803, when prayer meetings began in a barn in Birmingham Street. The church was built at a cost of £800. Not all the members were poor people but raising the funds necessary proved very difficult. The church, or meeting house as it was then called, was plain and decorous inside: the only thing between the pews and the high wide ceiling with its five decorated ventilators was the pulpit at the north end. The exterior was also plain, although the window arches with their specially moulded bricks broke the uniformity of the brick courses.

Demolition of the Congregational chapel, Hagley Street, 8 July 1960. In 1950 the building was listed as a building of historic or architectural importance, but it was demolished as a result of the Halesowen Borough Development Plan, a new church being erected in front of the Congregational hall in Hagley Road. The last wedding to be held in the church was that of Derek Hadley and Annette Cooper on 19 September 1959. And although public worship had already ceased in the building, it was especially re-opened on 9 April 1960 for the funeral of Bryan Cole, a fifteen year old who died tragically as a result of an accident. (*Michael Dancer*)

Stone-laying, Congregational hall, Hagley Road, June 1909. Numerous stones were laid inscribed with names, and many of these are still visible today. Mrs F.T. Danks of Quinton performed the opening ceremony of the hall on 28 February 1910.

The Revd F. W. Fisher of Suffolk in 1861, the fourth minister of the Congregational church (1855–60). His ministry does not appear to have been a very happy one: at one time he thought of going to Australia for mission work. In 1859 his ministerial stipend was increased to £120 per annum. Mr Fisher lived at Spring Villa, probably close to Thomas Harris's button factory in Spring Hill. Under his ministry the membership rose by sixty-two new members, among them George Granger and Henry Parrish.

Hasbury Methodist church, Wall Well, 1966. This building was the immediate forerunner of the present Hasbury Methodist church, but it was a little further along the road on the corner of Wall Well and Albert Road. The Society at Hasbury had been founded in 1831 in a cottage in Cherry Tree Lane. Eventually a stone structure was built, and this was replaced by the building in the photograph in 1861. The site had a beautiful situation, commanding a magnificent view of hill and dale. This building was replaced in 1970.

Interior of Hasbury Methodist church, *c.* 1970. The photograph is of the interior of the church, which was demolished in 1970. It shows the pulpit, behind which sat the choir and the organist. Below the pulpit is the communion area.

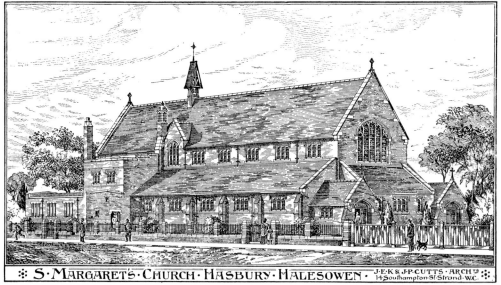

An original architect's sketch, showing how it was envisaged the new St Margaret's church at Hasbury would look. The foundation stone was laid on Wednesday 1 May 1907 by the Viscountess Cobham, and the church, which cost £4,000 to build, was dedicated for public worship in the presence of a large congregation by the Lord Bishop of Worcester on Monday 3 February 1908. The land had been given by Viscount Cobham of Hagley Hall and was valued at £400. The builders were W. Hopkins of Thorp Street, Birmingham, the clerk of the works was a Mr Priest and the architects were J.E.K. and J.P. Cutts, 14 Southampton Street, The Strand, London.

Short Cross Primitive Methodist church, Attwood Street, *c.* 1930. The Primitive Methodist cause at Short Cross began in 1867, when members were very likely meeting in homes. On 12 March 1868 the present site was purchased for £44 4*s*, and a schoolroom was erected. In 1891 the church was built, foundation stones being laid by B. Hingley Esq., MP and F.D. Lea-Smith Esq., CC on 11 May 1891. The building erected is the one featured in the photograph, and it continued to be used as the church until the present one was built in 1934. The 1891 building then became the Sunday School room, and served until it was demolished in 1976.

...de Service at Short Cross Methodist church, 1978. It is thought that the occasion was Ladies' Day.

Halesowen Methodist church, Birmingham Street, *c.* 1955. The Primitive Methodist cause at Birmingham Street goes back to 1840, with a chapel being erected in 1848. In 1868 the building in the photograph, still standing today, was started. The Primitive Methodist magazine of the day reported: 'Halesowen – A splendid chapel is in course of erection. The trustees have worked well in raising £100 for the site of land and £50 more at the stone laying. The chapel will be the finest and neatest building in the town.' In the early 1980s the church joined with the United Reformed to form the Halesowen United church. (*Phil Waldren*)

Sir Benjamin Hingley Bart MP (1830–1905). Sir Benjamin lived at Hatherton Lodge, Drews Holloway, and was the son of Noah Hingley of N. Hingley & Sons (Netherton) Ltd, the ironworks. He was the Liberal MP for the North Worcestershire Division, which included Halesowen, from 1885 to 1895. He was also a Halesowen Justice of the Peace from 1876 until his death. He was a benefactor to local churches, and he laid the foundation stone to the Birmingham Street Methodist chapel schoolroom on 26 August 1889 when he was Mayor of Dudley. The stone has now been re-sited inside the building, which is used as a restaurant called Benjamin's.

The memorial stone laid by Benjamin Hingley on 5 September 1892 at the building of the schoolroom at the Zion chapel in Cemetery Lane. He also laid one at Short Cross Methodist church schoolroom on 11 May 1891. Alderman Hingley laid a similar stone at the Birmingham Street Methodist church on 25 March 1868. This, though, was very likely Noah Hingley, the father of Benjamin, who was himself Mayor of Dudley from 1869 to 1870.

Short Cross Primitive Methodist church
Sunday School anniversary procession, 1899.
Left to right: Wilfred Dancer, aged thirteen,
James Coley, James Moore and John Dancer.

Hasbury and Halesowen Primitive Methodist circuit local preachers, 1914. Walter Seeley, who was a keen
photographer and produced some early Halesowen postcards, which he sold in his shop in Hagley Street:
he took this photograph at Romsley. Back row, left to right: H. Kindon, A. Taylor, D. Lee, H. Brittain,
G. Hadley, J.W. Kindon, J. Jones, J.B. Bissell. Middle row: G. Parkes, J. Higgs, a female helper,
W. Walker, Mrs Bath, A. Taylor, a female helper, H. Cole, B. Warr. Front row: A. Corbett, B. Timmins,
E. Price, J. Parkes, the Revd J. Humphries, R. Dorricott, ? Bate, J. Willetts, E. Timmins.

Halesowen Baptist church Sunday School treat, *c*. 1928. The dance around the maypole took place in Mr Hackett's field at Bundle Hill.

Zion Methodist church Sunday School anniversary, May 1955. Back row, left to right: Mr Attwood (organist) -?-, Mrs Dorothy Emery. Fourth row: Michael Rudge, Bryan Kite, Enid Emery, Susan Cooper, Jennifer Brittain. Third row: Keith White, Trevor Woodfield, -?-, Sylvia Knight, -?-, Carol McCulloch. Second row: Robert Hackett, Richard Kilby, Jean Woodfield, Pearl Kite, -?-, Pat Hepple, -?-. First row: Connie Allcock, Margaret Waldron, Ruby Wakeman, Winnie James, Margaret ?, the Revd Adam Chambers, -?-, Mrs Chambers, Jean Sawyer, Jack Emery. Standing to the left of the platform are Dennis Brittain and Bryan Allcock.

Short Cross Methodist church Men's Own, *c.* 1930. Football league champions and Coronation Cup winners, the Men's Own also had a choir. They played football on Saturdays and sometimes sang at the Short Cross Methodist church on Sundays. Back row, left to right: George Finch, George Attwood, Woodrow Bradley, Harry Williams, Jack Andrews. Front row: Edward Shilvock, Walter Franklin, Geoff Coley, Geoff Willetts, Geoff Willetts, Cyril Chapman, Geoff Sawyer, Arthur Coley, Edward Chapman, Jeffrey Coley.

Zion Methodist church Women's Own golden jubilee celebrations, 1978. The Zion Women's Own was the first such class to be formed in the town, and at one time had over eighty members. Back row, left to right: Miss F. Sawyer, Mrs G. Taylor, Mrs M. Hobday, Mrs E. Hackett. Front row: Mrs F. Allen, the Revd A.G. Trevithick and Mrs Sylvia Rudge. Mrs Hackett shortly afterwards celebrated her hundredth birthday, and Mrs Rudge was in her nineties. (*County Express*)

Short Cross Methodist church, Attwood Street,
October 1976. The 1891 church building
standing next door to the present church was
being demolished.

Former Shenstone Methodist church, Birmingham Road, 1966. This church was used for public worship
during the period 1894 to 1959. It was then used for trade purposes until it was demolished to make way
for the Shenstone island at the foot of Mucklow Hill.

Short Cross Methodist church Sunday School anniversary, 1977.

Opening of new church buildings at Short Cross Methodist church to replace the 1891 building, 27 January 1979. The Solicitor General the Rt Hon. Peter Archer MP is pictured performing the opening ceremony. With him are the Revd Christopher Hughes-Smith Chairman of the Birmingham Methodist District, the Mayor of Dudley, Councillor Sydney Fairfold, and the Revd A.G. Trevithick, Superintendent Minister of the Halesowen Circuit.

The former Manse in Lyde Green, Cradley, 1966. It is believed that in this house the hymn 'Wise Men Seeking Jesus' was written by the Revd James Thomas East. Mr East had to walk though the rural lanes of Cradley and Wollescote to conduct services, and it is believed that this inspired the verse of the hymn: 'In our fertile cornfields, while the sheaves are bound, in our busy markets, Jesus may be found.'

Halesowen Baptist church garden party, held at the home of the Revd A.H. Smith, in Gower Road, 1949. The Mayoress of Halesowen, Mrs E.A. Rudge, is receiving flowers, and Miss Daisy Moore is encouraging another child. Standing in the distance is Mr Ken Jackson.

Procession of witness organised by the Halesowen and Blackheath Methodist churches to mark the 250th anniversary of the conversion of John Wesley, 24 May 1988. This shows the procession along Earlsway, having left the Earls High School to proceed to the Leasowes, where Wesley visited, for an open air rally. The Blackheath churches processed down Mucklow Hill to the Leasowes.

The procession featured in the photograph above proceeds up Mucklow Hill, led by the Bishop of Dudley, the Rt Revd Anthony C. Dumper, and the Revd David Clarke, Halesowen Methodist Superintendent Minister.

The Rt Revd J.C. Hill, DD, Bishop of Hulme, Rector of Halesowen, 1893–1909. Dr Hill was a forceful preacher, and Halesowen parish church used to be full to hear him. It was necessary to be there at 5.30 p.m. to secure a good seat for a 6.30 p.m. service. One lady was in such a rush to be there in good time that she forgot to remove her apron, and only noticed it when she looked down during the service.

The Revd Henry Charles Asgil Colvile MA, Canon of Worcester, and Rural Dean of Dudley, 1917. Rector of Halesowen 1917–36, he was popularly known as 'Dew Drop'!

Zion Methodist chapel cricket team, *c.* 1930s, photographed by Ernest Eades. Standing, left to right: Frank Allen, Arnold Sawyer, Bert Sawyer, Percy Hodgetts, Edwin James, Harry Slater (umpire) Joe White. Second row: Leslie Edmonds, Duncan Basterfield, George Hodgetts. Front row: Sid Williams, Ray Harris, Reginald Raybould, Harry Sawyer.

11th South Staffs Boys' Brigade Company (now 2nd Halesowen) at Short Cross Methodist church, 1966. Standing, left to right: Michael Andrews, Ron Frazer, Richard Greaves, Mr Jim Price (Captain), Neil Price, John Parry, Richard Blakemore. Middle row: Robert Price, Steven Shilvock, Tony Morton, John Barton, Nigel Slim, Nigel Bennett, Peter Baker, Richard Smith, Paul Williams. Seated: Terry Kirton, Robert Wilkinson, Dennis Perry, Tim Hazzell, Nicholas Kingett, Alan Beatrup, Gary Westwood, Gary Westwood, Derek Macklin, Alex Long.

CHAPTER THREE

SCHOOLS

A group of girls doing drill at the Halesowen Girls' Church School during the last century.
Behind them is the wall to the cemetery.

Thomas Fox (1815–78). He was headmaster of Halesowen National School for thirty-four years. There is a stained glass window in Halesowen parish church dedicated to his memory. It depicts the parables of the lost coin, the good shepherd and the return of the prodigal son.

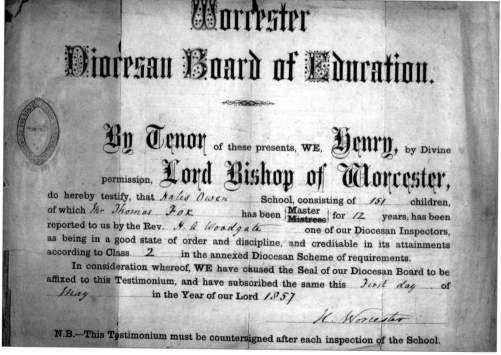

Testimonial on the state of Halesowen National (Church) Schools in 1857 – a kind of early Ofsted report!

A group of six-year-olds at Halesowen Church Schools, *c.* 1888. Second row up and fourth from the right is Alfred George Rudge of 9 Victoria Street. He became a local solicitor and Mayor of Halesowen 1949–50.

esowen Church Schools, 1910. Back row, left to right: Cliff Lashford, G. Shilvock, ? Grove, James Smith, ? Walker, eon Flo?, Hadley, Charley Hackett, Cliff Bradley, Ernie Brown, Lily ?. Second row: Mr Harris, Alice Jones, Lizzie nger, Florrie Jones, Iris ?, Daisy Jones, Kate Field, May Tether, Gladys Dingley, -?-, Clara Sawyer, Hilda Dearn, Abbiss (headmaster). Front row: ? Parsons, ? Lloyde, ? Connop, Albert Stanley, ? Attwood, Donald Stanley, ? Coley, nis Hackett, ? Goddard, Harvey Harrison, ? Shilvock, ? Parsons and Saul ?.

Hawne County Primary School, Stourbridge Road, 1966. Caleb Bloomer had erected this building in 1867 as the Islington Ragged Schools. Linden Glade now occupies the site but much of the boundary wall of the school fronting Stourbridge Road still remains. Newer buildings were erected behind the Ragged School in 1901 to house the infants of what by that time had become the British Schools. The school became Stourbridge Road County Primary School in 1908, and then eventually Hawne County Primary School. Bearing in mind that the school ceased to be the British School in 1908, it was still being called that by the locals when it closed in the mid-1980s.

A class group at the British Schools, c. 1907. Back row, left to right: Miss Harris, Rose Rudge, ? Brettle, Fred Morgan, ? Field, -?-, -?-, -?-, -?-, Miss Spencer. Third row: Edith Pardoe, John Bullas, Winnie Coley, Tom Goode, -?-, Clarence Greenhall, Lawson Slater, ? Hodgkins. Second row: -?-, ? Eden, -?-, ? Workman, ? Workman, ? Workman, Kathleen Maybury. Front row: Albert Greenhall, ? Hodgkins, ? Slater, ? Eden, Wesley Goode, ? Morgan.

Caleb Bloomer's Ragged School buildings, 1985 – just prior to demolition. The school was also used as a church on Sundays and weeknights. Caleb Bloomer died in 1872, and because there was disagreement over his will the school was closed, and it was eventually sold to the Primitive Methodists who ran a school there. Eventually it became the British Schools.

Caleb Bloomer's baptistry, 1985. In his Ragged Schools, Caleb Bloomer had a Baptistry sunk into the floor, and believers were baptised by total immersion. In his will Caleb bequeathed legacies to those who had been baptised. When the schools were demolished in the mid-1980s the old baptistry was found crumbling underneath the floorboards of the school hall.

Hasbury Church of England Infants School, 1920. Children are playing oranges and lemons; singing the well-known nursery rhyme, they start off in twos and catch the individual children with the words 'Here comes a candle to light you to bed, here comes a chopper to chop off your head'. A tug of war follows to prove whether it is the oranges or lemons who are the stronger. The third girl on left is Elsie Brettle, Phyllis Ray is between the two boys, and the boy in the middle of the girls on the right is Charles Brettle. Florence Macklin is the girl with the bow in her hair; to her left with a fringe is Dorothy Guest. Margaret Timmins is second on the left and Mary Moseley is the fourth child in from the right, with a ribbon in her hair.

Hasbury Church of England Infants School, 1920. The second girl on the left is Ariel Portman, fourth from the left is Vera Jones, eighth from the left is Kate Farley and to her right is Margaret Timmins. The boy on the extreme right is Harold Lea. The girl standing forward in the centre is Evelyn Layton.

Mr John James Shakespeare, one time headmaster of Colley Lane Primary School, Cradley. He lived two doors away from the school, and was a Halesowen Councillor who represented Halesowen West Ward from 1945 to 1954. John Shakespeare was from the Halesowen Shakespeare family who grew up in Laurel Lane. He was one of the five children of Charles Henry Shakespeare and Martha, *née* Dingley. He had two sisters, Margaret and Mary Ann, who married Hubert Rollason of Rollaprint. Mary taught at Lapal Primary School and was a local Methodist preacher. John's twin brothers were Tom and Charles: the latter worked in Bridge's butchers, Hagley Street.

Hasbury Church of England Infant School, *c.* 1930. Back row, left to right: Ivy Crumpton, Dorothy Lee, Hilda Holloway, Dorothy Coley, -?-, -?-, Nancy Moore, -?-, -?-. Second row: Kenneth Parkes, Arnold Field, ? James, -?-, Fred Bradley, Philip Shuker, -?-, Ray Williams, Dennis Jones. Third row: -?-, Eunice Ingram, Betty Grainger, Gwen Hadley, -?-, Barbara Tether. Seated on ground: Howard Bissell, -?-, -?-, Maurice Fox, Geoffrey Brittain, Eric Cole.

Stourbridge Road Junior School Standard 3, 1932. Back row, left to right: James Timmins, Douglas Harper, Leonard Garrish, Tom Cooper, Kenneth Hackett, Stan Coley, Arthur Coley, -?-, Desmond Jones. Fourth row: Gladys Sarson, Kathleen Brown, Edith Parkes, Beryl Woodhouse, Irene Worton, Elsie Jones, Margaret Brown, Joan Leashon, Doris Sambrooks, Mary Lowe, Irene Willetts. Third row: Hilda Partridge, -?-, -?-, Mabel Hackett, -?-, Peggy Williams, Eileen Moore, Margery Guest. Second row: -?-, Betty Butterworth, Joan Tibbetts. Front row: George Hart, Fred Lowe, -?-, Kenneth Cornfield, John Clift.

Stourbridge Road Junior School choir group, 1936. The choir was formed to sing at Halesowen Grammar School at a music festival organised by Billy Thomas. Back row, left to right: Colin Siviter, Edward Lowe (played for Fulham and Aston Villa football clubs as well as representing England), Raymond Rudge, Edward Nock, Frank Farley, George Stokes, Sydney Allen, Charles Greenwood, Andrew Sarson, Geoffrey Price, Geoffrey Evans. Third row: May Webster, Doris Slater, Miriam Hackett, Iris Male, Lilian Hart, Eileen Robinson, Pat Roberts, ? Weston. Second row: Margery Whyley, Nellie Watson, Dorothy Webster, Joan White, Irene James, Alice Davies. Front row: Stella Page, Madge Partridge, Hilda Brown, Jean Southwell, Doreen Moss.

Irene Willetts in a field on the Burma Road, now Whittingham Road, 1940. The field is where Newfield Primary School stands. During the war, and until the houses were built and the road was completed, it was always called Burma Road because its surface was like red sand with small boulders sticking out, and it was thought to be like the infamous road cut through the jungles of south-east Asia by Allied prisoners of war.

Class group at Halesowen Grammar School, 1922.

Halesowen Church of England School football team, 1939. Back row, left to right: Dennis Bennett, Arthur Connop, Ron Bissell, John Hulston, Laurence Bingham, Eric Tibbetts, Noel Webster. Second row: Donald James, Mr Lyes, Mr Wilson (headmaster) Mr Crampton, Clement Bissell. Front row: Harry Bennett and Douglas Webster.

Halesowen County Modern Boys' School football team, 1939, league champions. Back row, left to right: Mr Watkins (headmaster), Dennis Bennett, Noel Webster, Laurence Bingham, Harry Bennett, Rex Lashford, Mr Reason. Front row: Warren Bradley, Walter Walker, Reg Lowe, Ron Bissell, Donald James, Clement Bissell.

Rachel Basterfield, Rose Queen at the Rose Queen festival, Hasbury Church of England Infants School, *c*. 1954.

The Rose Queen, Rachel Basterfield, is escorted by David Rogers, who subsequently became Vicar of Cradley and is now Vicar of Beoley.

Stourbridge Road County Junior School Class 1, 1956. Back row, left to right: Bronte Andrews, Lesley James, Susan Wakefield, Ann Jackson, Ann Taylor, Ann Bradley, Joy Hyland, Sandra Faulkner, Judith Lay. Second row: Richard Ball, Paul Windsor, Derek Beasley, David Eades, Robert Hill, Robert Edgington, Michael Williams, Sydney Rudge, David Hough, Lesley Faulkner. Front row: Bruce Lakin, Kenneth Cox, Robert Oliver, Alan Hackett, Robert Sherlock, Mr George Berry, Jill Coley, Elaine Gadd, Margaret Mcgrath, Diane Allsop, Christine Crumpton.

A Christmas Carol, Hawne County Primary School, c. 1960. Back row, left to right: Sheila Davenport, Gail Tibbets, Jennifer Hackett, Susan Cooper, -?-, Phillip Tibbetts, Adrian Hackett, Jenny Williams (standing in front), Richard Blakemore, -?-, -?-, -?-, Judith Franklyn, -?-, -?-. Second row: Patricia Plant, Jennifer Rudge, Gillian Hackett, -?-, -?-, Jennifer Clift, Lynne Morgan, Jane Builder, Gillian Wood, -?-, -?-, Robert Faulkner, -?-, Neil Price. Front row: -?-, -?-, Stephen Hawkins, Phillip Hannan, Sheralyn Locke, Stewart Westwood, Christine Williams, -?-, -?-, -?-, -?-.

Halesowen County Secondary Modern Boys' School, Richmond Street, Christmas concert, December 1956. The choir was conducted by Alex Bryce.

...sowen County Secondary Modern Boys' School Class 1A, 1957. Back row, left to right: Mr Vernon G. Hale, Fred ...:on, John Shilvock, David Williams Anthony Brettle, David Eades, Alan Bunford, Royston Etheridge, Paul Taylor, ...ard Workman, David Symon. Second row: Chester Merris, Alan Gregory, David Bennett, John Bissell, Robert ..., Peter Humphries, James Orme, Alan Hadley, Ian Jeavons, Robert Hill. Front row: Ralph Cross, Harold Calder, ... Hodgetts, Keith Jones, Brian Withers, Ian Perkins, Brett Webster, Robert Webster, Bryan Cole, Robert Oliver, ... Bradney.

Halesowen College of Further Education, Secondary Technical School Department, fourth form class group, 1960. Back row, left to right: Gary Parkes, John Gwilliam, Michael Page, David Williams, John Whittaker, Lionel Parkes, David Prentice, Bernard Boden. Second row: David Cox, Michael Skelding, David Eades, Ian Jeavons, John Shilvock, Fred Detheridge, David Watson, Victor Marsh. Front row: John Taplin, Gilbert Cook, Keith Hussey, Terence Benton, Mr R Dumelow, Andrew Jones, John Westwood, Ian Perkins, David Symon.

Halesowen College of Further Education Staff Group, 1960. Back row, left to right: Mrs A.M. Wakefield, Miss Gregory, C.A. Round, J. McTier, B. Szmanski, J.F. Beasley, R.J. Dumelow, R. Brettell, J.W.D. Leaver, Mrs R.M. Ru Second row: Mrs G.M. Gardiner, Mrs K. Lynne, Mrs J.M. Avis, A.L. Hammonds, H. White, R. Greenway, G. G N. Holloway, Miss K. Wilson, Miss P.A. Marginson, Mrs E.J. James. Front row: Mrs E. Cheese, K.W. Limbird, M. Hughes, R.G. Harris, J.H. Simpson (Principal), J. Williams, Miss S. Downing, H.W. Graydon, Mrs N.E. Crampt

lesowen College of Further Education, Secondary Technical School Department, fourth form chemistry lesson. Left-
nd side of class, from back, left to right: Anthony Palmer, Bryan Cole, Keith Houghton, Michael Husband, Alan
dley, Colin Billington, John Owen, Right-hand side: Roger Watkins, David Parkes, David Hill, Mr R.J. Dumelow,
bin Brettell, Alan Reed, Robert Griffiths, David Eddleston, John Teese, Alan Broadbent, John Wyre, Peter
zlewood, Roger Cartwright.

group, Halesowen Grammar School, c. 1962. Back row, left to right: John Grigg, -?-, Michael Lay, -?-, ? Hodgetts,
Hughes, -?- , Roger Mann, Martin, -?-, -?-, Stephen Morley. Second row: Susan Cooke, Janis Marshall, Jacqueline
er, John Northwood, Geoffrey Ditchfield, Malcolm ?, Susan Cooper, Gillian Wills, Hilary James, Gillian Evans.
row: Susan ?, Margaret ?, Georgina South, Joyce ?, -?-, Gillian ?, -?-, Sarajane Searles.

Hasbury Church of England Infants School staff, *c.* 1951–2. Back row, left to right: Miss Kath Fox, Mrs Betty Worsdall. Front row: Miss Dorothy Sellars, Miss M.E. Fearnside, Miss Jean K. Grainger, Miss Oakes.

Grammar School Lane, 1966. The photograph was taken from the Halesowen Borough Hall, now Borough Court. Buildings to the left stood to the right of the existing gate to the Earls High School and were formerly the Kindergarten. Further along was the new Drill Hall.

Halesowen Church Schools, 1966. This photograph was taken before the building was modernised.

The Ministry of Labour, Old Hawne Lane, 1966. Originally the building was the Technical School. It was closed in 1939 when the new Technical College opened in Furnace Lane, with Johnson Ball as Principal. The buildings are now part of the Borough Court complex.

The new Halesowen College of Further Education under construction in Whittingham Road, 1966.

ew buildings under construction at the County Secondary Modern Boys' School, Richmond Street, 1966.

nty Secondary Modern Girls' School, Bundle Hill, 1966.

Huntingtree Primary School, Bournes Hill, 1966. The Mayor of Halesowen, Councillor Norman Garner, official opened the school on 10 July 1958. The Rector of Halesowen, the Revd Patrick Blakiston, dedicated the buildings. T builders were Cooper & Son, West Street, Blackheath, General Foreman was B. Guest and Clerk of Works w G.J. Deakin.

Hawne Primary School, Stourbridge Road, 1966. A class of children first occupied the flat-roofed building to the rig 1950. Beyond can be seen the houses in Old Hawne Lane, before the ambulance station and the Brett Young Centre built.

CHAPTER FOUR

CIVIC LIFE

The original Grant of Arms to the Borough Of Halesowen in 1936. It is signed at the foot by Garter King of Arms and Clarenceux and Norroy Kings of Arms.

A civic event at Halesowen bandstand in Highfields Park, *c.* 1914. Note the arms of the Halesowen Urban Dist Council. At the entrance to the bandstand is Arthur Timmins, the Halesowen builder and undertaker, with his daug Joyce – who died of diphtheria aged five in 1914. It is not known what the event is but could it be the opening of the bandstand?

Menu for the last dinner for Halesowen Council as an Urban District. The evening was arranged so that the Charter Mayor could acknowledge the gifts of civic regalia and many other items which were given when Halesowen became a Borough. The gifts included the mace from the Halesowen Steel Company, the mayor's chain and badge from Walter Somers Ltd, the Mayor's occasional badge, from Mr and Mrs Hipkiss, the mayoress's chain from Stewarts and Lloyd's Ltd, and the deputy mayor's badge from Mr and Mrs Jas Oakley. The musical programme was provided by the Blue Ricardo Band, with Miss Gladys Slater (soprano) as vocalist.

The dinner was held at the Masonic Hall, 27 August 1936. The top table was along the right-hand side in front of the Masonic boards and windows, and the VIPs were, left to right: Mr Seth Somers, Mr and Mrs H.J. Cox (Deputy Charter Mayor and Mayoress), Mr and Mrs J.B. Downing (Charter Mayor and Mayoress), Alf Basterfield (Charter Town Clerk) and Mrs Basterfield, Mr T. Smith (Chairman of the Council) and Mrs Smith, Mr A.G. Rudge (Vice-Chairman of the Council) and Mrs Rudge, Mr W. Green. (*County Express*)

County Alderman J.B. Downing OBE, JP, the Charter Mayor of Halesowen. Alderman Downing owned a factory in New Road, J.B. Downing Ltd. He served as a councillor on the Halesowen Rural District Council from 1907 to 1925, and was Chairman from 1915 to 1916 and 1923 to 1924. He served as an Urban District Councillor throughout the life of the Council, 1925–36, and was its Chairman from 1927 to 1928, and 1934 to 1935. He was an alderman on the Borough Council from 1936 until his death in 1941, and was Mayor of the Borough from 1936 to 1938. Mr Downing was appointed as a Justice of the Peace for the town in 1922.

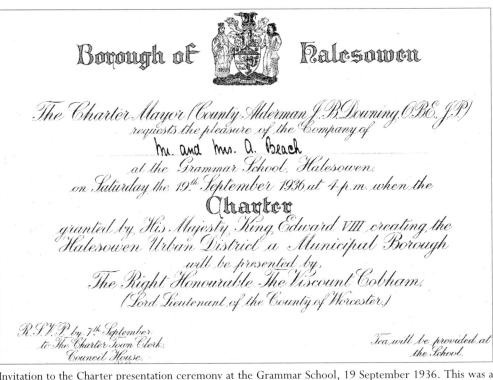

Invitation to the Charter presentation ceremony at the Grammar School, 19 September 1936. This was a big day in the life of the town with processions leaving Cradley, Hill and Cakemore and the town centre to form up at the Grammar School to provide a Guard of Honour. A procession of twenty-four cars left for the Borough boundary at Hayley Green to meet Lord Cobham, Lord Lieutenant of the County of Worcester. The procession then made its way to the Grammar School for the formal ceremony. The Band of the 7th Battalion, the Worcestershire Regiment, played.

Ox roasting at the Grove Recreation Ground to celebrate the Coronation of King George VI and Queen Elizabeth, 1937.

The Spitfire purchased by the people of Halesowen in November 1940, at a cost of £5,000. It commenced its operational career in April 1942, and was engaged upon fighter sweeps, bombers' escorts and convoy patrol. On one occasion the squadron to which it belonged attacked a goods train at Le Treport and left the two engines damaged. In August 1942, after taking part in an air attack on targets in occupied France, the Spitfire was shot down.

The opening of Manor Abbey Sports Ground by Sydney Wooderson, the famous British mile record holder, of Blackheath Harriers, in front of a crowd of approximately three thousand, 6 August 1949. The photograph shows, left to right, Mr Wooderson, Mr S. Smith, the Mayor of Halesowen (Councillor A.G. Rudge) addressing the people, Seth Somers, Mr R.K. Brown, -?- and Bernard Bray. (*Birmingham Post*)

Opening of the Midland Counties Dairy Depot at Long Lane, Hill and Cakemore by the Mayor of Halesowen, Councillor A.G. Rudge, accompanied by the Mayoress, Mrs E.A. Rudge. Also present were the Mayor and Mayoress of Rowley Regis, Alderman and Mrs G. Palmer.

Welfare Foods meeting at the Council Chamber, 9 November 1949. Mr J.W. Cooper, the Food Executive Officer, said that the Government had decided to look after the children of the country by laying plans to ensure the safety of mothers and babies. The Welfare Foods Service was the result of this step. Dr Corlett said that twenty years before rickets had been a common occurrence, but because of the vitamin foods provided it was now very rare, and no child today had a really bad start in life. He emphasised that every child should have proper food, early hours and plenty of fresh air.

Scene outside Long Lane Library, when the Mayor of Halesowen, Councillor W. Parkes, read the proclamation of the ascension to the throne of Her Majesty Queen Elizabeth II, 1952.

The Queen and the Duke of Edinburgh drive along Hagley Street past the Bulls Head and the Chocolate Box Café on th
visit to the town, 23 April 1957.

Halesowen Public Library and Council Chamber decorated for the visit of the Queen to the town on
23 April 1957.

Presentation of badges to past mayoresses, Council Chamber, 28 January 1959. Standing, left to right: Alderman F.L. Rose, Mrs B. Rose, Mrs P. Scott, Councillor P.W. Scott (Deputy Mayor), Mrs A.H. Spring, Mrs N. Garner (Mayoress), Councillor Norman Garner (Mayor), Miss D. Parkes, Mr J.B. McCooke (Town Clerk), Mrs G.A, Southall, Mrs J.R. Poole, Alderman C. Willetts, Alderman G. Southall. Seated: Mrs H.J. Cox, Mrs J.B. Downing, Mrs A.G. Rudge, Mrs C. Willetts.

...rmen, councillors and council officials on the occasion of the last meeting of the Council for the municipal year ...8–9. Back row, left to right: -?-, -?-, T.N.E. Smith (Librarian), A.W. Parker (Treasurer), Mrs Bennett (Mayor's ...etary), -?-, Miss. E. Dallard (Housing Manager), T.W. Tivey (Engineer and Surveyor), Dr L. Corlett (Medical ...cer), A. Archer (Public Health Inspector). Second row: Councillors W.J. Cadd, A.H. Neale, C.R. Tromans, ...Field, D.C. Herbert, Mrs E. Smith, Mr Dunn (Mace Bearer), Councillors A. Whitehouse, R. Blakeway, Miss ...Bridge, H. Davies, P. Timmins, L. Hughes, A.H. Spring. Front row: Aldermen C. Willetts, L. Harper, F.L. Rose, ...McCooke (Town Clerk), Councillor Norman Garner (Mayor), Councillor P.W. Scott (Deputy Mayor), the Vicar of ...heath, the Revd W.J.C. Farmer (Mayor's Chaplain), Aldermen W. Hodgetts and G.A. Southall.

Civic Sunday, May 1973: the beginning of the last year in the life of Halesowen as a Borough. The newly elected Mayor, Councillor Frank Price, processes to Halesowen parish church for the civic service. He is preceded by the Mace Bearer Mr Jim Hackworth, and flanked on his right by the Town Clerk, Mr J.B. McCooke, and on his left by his Chaplain, the Revd Gordon W. Wood. (*Peter Barnsley*)

The last civic service for the Borough of Halesowen, 31 March 1974. The following day the Borough of Halesowen became part of the Metropolitan Borough of Dudley. The Mayor of Halesowen, surrounded by councillors, officials and guests, takes the salute as the parade passes the Council House.

CHAPTER FIVE

INDUSTRY, EVENTS & PERSONALITIES

The Homfray family, Otterbourne Court, Bundle Hill, c. 1900. Standing, left to right: Jeston Homfray, Millicent Homfray, Dr Alex McMillan, Alfred Homfray, Frank Somers, Reginald Homfray. Seated: Kathleen Homfray, Mrs Alfred Homfray, Kenyon Homfray. Mr Alfred Homfay, who had Otterbourne Court built, was a local solicitor and was Clerk to the Halesowen Justices from 1895 to 1934. Kathleen Homfray married Frank Somers. The Homfray forebears, Jeremiah and Samuel Homfray, founded the Penydarren Ironworks, Merthyr Tydfil, and in 1804 Richard Trevithick built the first steam locomotive to run on rails for Samuel Homfray.

Miss Lillian Amy Lea-Smith of The Grange, daughter of Ferdinando Dudley Lea-Smith and his wife Amy Sophia, who was the granddaughter of Sir Oswald Mosley Bart. When her father died in 1905 Miss Lea-Smith, who travelled the world, was anxious to receive her inheritance, so the Waxlands fields had to be sold. The family did not stay long in Halesowen following this.

Elizabeth, second wife of Ferdinando Smith JP, DL of The Grange. Halesowen. Elizabeth was the fourth daughter of Michael Grazebrook of Audnam. She had four children including two sons who died in infancy, George and Henry Lea-Smith. Ferdinando Dudley Lea-Smith, born on 15 June 1834, and William Lea-Smith, born on 27 February 1836, survived.

The home of Sam Williams, The Drive, Halesowen, 1905. Mr Williams owned the Crown Perambulator factory. Left to right: Mrs Leek, Ethel Ferraby, Phyllis Williams, Gladys Williams, Mrs Rhoda Williams.

Ferdinando Dudley Lea-Smith (born 15 June 1834, died 8 February 1905), of The Grange, Halesowen. Mr Lea-Smith was educated at Eton and Christchurch, Oxford. He was called to the Bar at The Inner Temple on 26 January 1858. He was High Sheriff of the County of Worcester, a Halesowen Justice of the Peace and Chairman of the Bench from about 1884 until his death in 1905. A Lea-Smith charity was active from about 1845 to 1904. Coats for men and gowns for women were given to the poor of the town. Among the recipients in 1873 were Thomas Crumpton (blind) of Hasbury, William Williams of Love Lane, Dinah Walker of Gaunts Fold and Jane Faddington of Towns End.

Works outing from Grove's button factory, *c.* 1919. Standing third from the right is James Ferraby. He was apprentic 1887 for three years for learning the trade of making ivory and horn buttons.

George Rudge of Victoria Street, wearing the chain of office of Grand Master of the National United Order of Free Gardeners, *c*. 1910. The order was a friendly society, which existed at the turn of the century. It was very strong in the Black Country and locally there were 193 branches in 1906. Mr Rudge was secretary of the Trafalgar Wreath Lodge No. 1147, which dated back to 1875 when its registered offices were at the Star Inn. In December 1911 it had a membership of 342 and funds of £1,642.

Two Halesowen families joined in matrimony on 27 August 1899, at St Peter and St Paul's church in the parish of Aston. Ernest George Eades of Laurel Lane and Mercy Price of Cemetery Lane, Halesowen, were married from the home of the bridegroom's sister. Left to right: Roseannah Turner (*née* Eades), Ernest George Eades, Mercy Price, John Fox Turner, -?-.

The wedding of Harriet Annie Rudge of Victoria Street and Albert Percy Herbert of Langley, who were married at Halesowen parish church by the Rector of Halesowen, the Revd Ronald Symes MA, on 20 October 1909. Percy Herbert came from a journalistic family. His father, Henry, served in the profession for forty years and his elder brother, A.H. Herbert, was a journalist and newspaper proprietor for fifty-one years. Percy started in journalism in 1892, and he became the correspondent for the Halesowen, Rowley Regis and Oldbury districts for the *County Express* and the *Birmingham Post* and *Mail*. He was also a correspondent for the national newspapers.

Percy and Harriet Annie Herbert with their son Albert Rex, *c.* 1920. Rex was articled in Law to his uncle, the Halesowen and Brierley Hill solicitor A.G. Rudge. He gained third class honours in his final examination in 1932, and was awarded a special prize by the Birmingham Law Society for being one of only three candidates in the Midlands to gain honours that year. Rex was Clerk to Chertsey Urban District Council in Surrey for many years.

George Beers (22 July 1856–19 August 1929).
Born George Beere at North End, Burton
Dassett, Warwickshire, he came to Halesowen
when he was eighteen. George was a ganger
with the Midland Railway. He married Mary
Ann Brown of the shovel works family: she did
not like his surname, so he altered it to Beers.
They lived at Romsley for some years and
George was a member of the Hunnington Parish
Council. For over forty years George was a
Primitive Methodist local preacher but
subsequently joined the Congregational church
where he was president of the Christian
Endeavour.

side the Fox Hunt public house, Hayley Green, 1892. This was taken before the black and white façade was attached
he building, which made people think the public house was really older than it actually was. When the building was
olished to make way for the present edifice, the brickwork revealed was exactly as in this picture. The lady in the
tograph is Mrs Emma Jane Fox. Charles Fox is holding the cat and his daughter Nellie is standing by him. The others
e group are locals.

Edward Gem JP. Mr Gem lived at Belle Vue, at the top of Mucklow Hill. He was a local businessman and a Justice of the Peace. He was churchwarden at Halesowen parish church from 1859 to 1861. He died in 1905.

Dr Edward Moore FRCS, JP. Edward Moore was a Sedgley man, but after studying medicine at St Bartholomew's Hospital, London, he came to Halesowen and stayed for the rest of his life. He lived at Townsend House, which eventually became the Conservative Club. He was a Justice of the Peace for Worcestershire and Staffordshire, and was Deputy Lieutenant for Worcestershire. Dr Moore was churchwarden at Halesowen parish church and the lancet window above the west door was erected in 1875 to his memory. His son, General Sir William Moore, was appointed Honorary Physician to Queen Victoria in 1888.

The coal strike, 1926. When the coal strike was under way the railway men came out in sympathy, and Mr Garratt, the owner of New Hawne Colliery, gave the poor folks permission to pick their own coal. Standing, left to right: Mrs Anne Guest, Guy Walker, Mr Walker snr.

The Coal Strike, 1926. The people were allowed to pick coal at New Hawne Colliery. From left to right: Mrs Field, holding Charles Parson, Mrs Shilvock, Mary Guest (who later became Mrs Millington), Mrs Elizabeth Cooper, holding her son Frederick Thomas, and Mr Tibbetts from Bloomfield Street, who reared pigs and horses and was known as Shady. Mrs Cooper lived off the Burma Road, in Gypsy Lane.

Mr Caleb Smith and family of Bloomfield Street. Mr Smith formerly kept the off-licence in Bloomfield Street. Behind him are his three daughters: Jesse (left) and Bridget (middle), but unfortunately the name of the third is unknown. Mr Smith's headgear is thought to be a smoker's hat, worn when clay pipes were smoked. It was either navy blue or black.

J. Arthur Guest, pictured with a radio that he had built himself, 1929.

Halesowen fire brigade practising at Huntingtree, 1920. The Captain on the extreme left is James Parkes. He lived with his wife in the old Council House in Cornbow which housed the fire engine. The old Council House long since demolished stood opposite the present Council House and had little Dutch gables. The Council moved to Cornbow House (the present Council House) in 1930.

Halesowen Band photographed at the home of the Grove family, St Margaret's Well House, Quarry Lane, when the bandstand was opened at Highfields Park, *c.* 1914.

The Twelfth Baron Dudley, Ferdinando Dudley William Lea-Smith of the Grange, Halesowen. He served in the South African War 1901–2, was appointed a magistrate the year in which his father died, 1905, and was Lieutenant-Colonel in the 6th Battalion the Worcestershire Regiment from 1911 to 1916. He was responsible for calling the title Baron Dudley, first created in 1439, out of abeyance in 1916. His son Ferdinando Dudley Henry Lea-Smith died without issue, so his daughter Barbara Amy Felicity is the present Baroness Dudley. Lord Dudley's coming of age in 1893 was fully covered in the *County Express*, and during the day the parish bells rang merry peals to celebrate the event.

Worcestershire Regiment soldiers in Wiltshire, *c.* 1916. They were undergoing training prior to going to France. The soldier seated on the extreme right is John Tranter of Spring Cottage, The Drive. John worked in the bolt trade. He was a football enthusiast and for some years was secretary of the Hasbury club. In France he belonged to the machine-gun section. Nothing more was heard of him after the offensive on the Somme on 24 April 1917. He has no known grave but is commemorated on the Thiepval Memorial. John was engaged to be married to Miss Ethel Beers, who died of a broken heart, it is said, in 1920.

Lance-Corporal George Eden, who lost his life in the First World War and whose name is recorded on Short Cross Methodist church's memorial as well as being inscribed on Halesowen's war memorial.

The wedding of Arthur Beach and Francis Fox, July 1931. Arthur was a well-known figure in Halesowen, as a member of St Margaret's church, Hasbury, and one-time churchwarden, and Company Secretary at Halesowen Steel Works. Mr and Mrs Beach lived in St Kenelm's Avenue.

Samuel Siviter, Nailer of Islington (1835–1910). He enlisted for the Grenadier Regiment of the Foot Guards on 3 July 1854 at Newcastle under Lyme. The portrait is an oil painting and was painted by his officer, to whom he was batman. Samuel was in No. 6 Company of the 2nd Battalion of the Grenadier Guards. He was stationed at various locations in London, including Portman Street, which was used for the mounting of the Royal Guard and the Tower of London, and also saw service in Dublin. An entry in his pay book of 'No. of Rifles 450' may indicate that he was in charge of the battalion armoury.

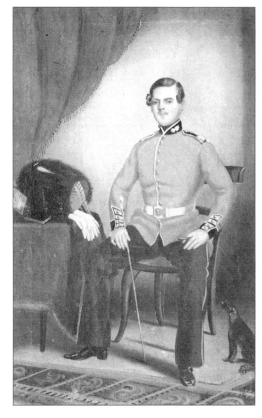

The soldier on the right is Sergeant Claude Rose in the Halesowen Company of 1/7 Worcesters. The photograph shows Claude at camp in 1913. He served in Belgium and France during the First World War and was awarded the Distinguished Conduct Medal for patrol work at Ploegsteert (Plugstreet) Wood near Ypres, and then the Somme.

VE Day party at Margaret Avenue, 1945. The photograph was taken by Ernest George Eades.

Short Cross football team, 1953. Standing, left to right: Stan Rudge, Malcolm Jackson, -?-, Vernon Hall, Laur-
Bingham, Ken Shuker, Ken ?, Derek Hall, Geoff Willetts. Front row: Colin Price, -?-, Ken Totney, -?-, Pat Carroll, -?

Walter Somers (1839–1917). Walter was born at Repton, south-west of Derby, and came to Halesowen in 1867 when he leased Haywood Ironworks. This was the beginning of Walter Somers Ltd, and the long and philanthropic connection that the Somers family has had with the town. Walter Somers was appointed a Justice of the Peace for the town in 1898, to be followed in those footsteps by his two sons, Seth and Frank. Walter Somers was the first Chairman of the Halesowen Rural District Council when it was formed in 1894, an office he held for four years. He lived in Mount Bromsgrove Street and at Belle Vue, at the top of Mucklow Hill.

Halesowen St John Ambulance Brigade Nursing Division, 1939/40. Back row, left to right: -?-, Miss H. Bidmead, -?-, Miss M.E. Fearnside, Miss Knowles, Miss M. Bridge, -?-, Elsie ?. Middle row: Miss Basterfield, Miss L. Sawyer, Miss Bridge, Mrs E. Cooper, Miss F. Sawyer, Mrs Pangelly, Mrs Willetts, -?-, Miss Knowles, Mrs M. Lamb, Mrs Searancke. Front row: Mrs Marshall-Mead, Dr Bold, the Mayor of Halesowen, Alderman H.J. Cox, the Mayoress, Mrs H.J. Cox, Miss Ashton, Mrs Skidmore.

Miss Gladys Slater (later Mrs G. Tilley) lived at Hill and Cakemore, and was the lead soprano for the BBC Radio Singers. She was very well known in the district and sang at many functions and charity concerts in the area. She topped the bill at the opening celebrity concert at the Rex Cinema, Blackheath, on Sunday 25 September 1938. Other soloists on that occasion were Austin Penzer, Joseph Farrington and Harry Pell.

Victor and Emma Hodgkins of Hilston Avenue. Mrs Hodgkins was a familiar sight around Halesowen with her spaniels. Mr Hodgkins owned the hoop factory in Bloomfield Street West, commonly called 'The Chip Yard'. Three hundred and fifty years ago Hodgkins made hoops in Birmingham Street but by 1855 the factory had been transferred to Short Cross. At that time it was one of several hundred hoop works in the country, but the number dwindled until the Halesowen factory was the last remaining. The name 'chip yard' arose because the waste wooden chips were stored in barrels, and the locals used them for fires as they lit easily.

The Hayley Green Joint Hospital Board at the opening of the hospital, *c.* 1900. The Chairman, Mr Whitehouse of Whitehouse's Foundry, is standing in the middle of the front row.

The last meeting of the Hayley Green Hospital Committee, 1948. The photograph was taken in front of the Nurses' Home, which was built in 1947 as a memorial to the Battle of Britain in 1940, and was called 'The Battle' by the nurses. Standing, left to right: -?-, Mr Folkes, Mr W. Guest, Mr A.G. Rudge, Mr F.H. Grove, -?-, -?-, Dr Corlett. Seated: Mr Folkes, Miss Grove, -?-, Mrs Lunt, Mr T. Smith, Sir George Eddy, Matron Jones, Mrs Francis, Miss Moody, -?-, Mr A.P. Herbert.

Frank Somers OBE, JP (1882–1965). Frank Somers was the second son of Walter Somers, and he succeeded his brother Seth as chairman of the company in 1955. He was educated at Halesowen Grammar School and was awarded the OBE in 1919 in recognition of his firm's work during the First World War. He was appointed a Justice of the Peace in 1918, becoming Chairman of the Bench from 1947 to 1949. In 1957, with Dr James Milroy McQueen, he was made one of the first Freemen of the Halesowen Borough. Frank was a great benefactor but will be best remembered for the first attempt to write a definitive history of Halesowen, which he and his daughter Kathleen published in 1932: it was entitled *Halas, Hales, Halesowen*.

The Old Brigade football team, *c.* 1900. On the extreme right of the back row, the man with whiskers is very likely Jos Beach, landlord of the Heart in Hand (later the King Edward), treasurer and financier of the team. The man next to him in a bowler hat is probably William Adams, team secretary and school teacher. Third from the left is A.G. Rudge.

Eric George Price, 1984. Mr Price worked in the courts service in Halesowen for nearly fifty years, being appointed Clerk to the Justices in 1959 – a position he held until 1985 when he retired, combining it with the Clerkship of Stourbridge from 1974. On his retirement the Halesowen magistrates held a special dinner in his honour, at which presentations were made. On his last day in court many tributes were paid. Paul Shaw said, speaking on behalf of the town's solicitors and quoting Shakespeare: 'We shall not see his like again'. (*County Express*)

Arthur Timmins, the local undertaker and builder, photographed in Hagley Street outside the house which eventually became the MEB showroom, and was demolished during the town centre redevelopment.

Stewart and Lloyd's ladies bowls team, 1950. Front row, left to right: Vera Shufflebotham, A. Rushton, Gladys Whittl[...] J. Sawyer, Madge Kite, Margaret Parsons, Connie Priest. Standing: M. Hatfield, Winnie Partridge, -?-, Sheila James, -[...] -?-, ? Lee, -?-, Rita Rushton, Iris ?, -?-. (F.J. Tromans)

Stewart and Lloyd's amateur dramatics group performing *Today of All Days*, 1950s. Gladys Bispham was playe[...] Margaret Parsons. Left to right: John Grice (standing), Jack Clarke (seated), Mary Williams, Madge Kite, Gl[...] Whittle, Margaret Parsons. (F.J. Tromans)

Halesowen Steel Works, Mucklow Hill. The stack was a familiar landmark. Between the war years the company continued to grow, and again in the Second World War it played a large part in producing steel for different elements of the war effort. It reached an annual production at that time of over 30,000 tons.

The head offices of Halesowen Steel Company, Mucklow Hill. The firm, incorporated in 1908, was one of the first in the Midlands to produce bright drawn steel bars. During the First World War it worked very closely with the Government in producing special steels to help the war effort, and produced 35 per cent of the whole of the bright steel required from this country for shell parts, aeroplane and flying boat engines and fittings, tank accessories and so on.

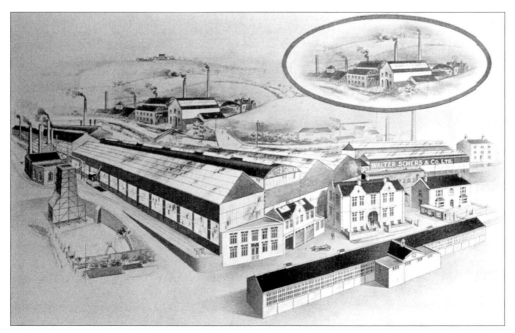

A bird's-eye view of Walter Somers Ltd, 1919. On the horizon is the home of Walter Somers, Belle Vue, at the top of Mucklow Hill, from where he could keep a watchful eye on his works!

General offices, Walter Somers Ltd, Prospect Place, 1919.

Dancers shop, Hagley Street, 1950s.

Board meeting, Halesowen Steel Company. Mr Arthur Beech, Company Secretary, is pictured on the extreme left.

The interior of Walter Somers' factory shell plant, 1916. The women are engaged in the production of 9.2 in shells for the First World War. The lady operating the crane is Gerty Grainger, and the lady second from the left is Eliza Grainger.

The remains of New Hawne Colliery, near to Hayseech, mid-1970s. (*Peter Barnsley*)

The workforce at Whitehouse's Foundry, Stourbridge Road. Mr Whitehouse, the owner, is seated in the centre of the front row, with a son either side of him – Fred to the left. On the extreme left of the back row is Mr Clissett. Second row and fourth from the right is Mr Edge. On the third row, extreme left, is Dennis Brittain, and on his left is William Eades; fifth from the right on the same row is a Mr Whitehouse, the lorry driver, with Jimmy Bath second from the right. On the front row, extreme left, is (?) Ernest Fellows, and to his left Jimmy Dock.

Colliers at the Coombes Wood Colliery, c. 1920. The colliery was roughly in the area where Makro is situated today. (*Peter Barnsley*)

ACKNOWLEDGEMENTS

Special thanks to Peter Barnsley, Ron and Jean Basterfield, Laurie and Marje Bingham, Alan and Margaret Bissell, Irene and Eric Brittain, Dorothy Carr, Kate Cole, Gill and Eric Collins, Michael Dancer, Gerald Darby, Edith Faulkner, Norman Fitchett, Jackie Garbett, Jean Grainger, Brian and Judith Green, Edna Griffin, Arthur Guest, Joyce Hackett, Jean Hadley, Derek Hadley, Michael Hall, Lyndon Harris, Stan Hill, Geoff Hodgetts, Norman Jones, Eileen Manning, Margaret and George Morley, Margaret Roberts, Ernest Rose, Evelyn Russell, Susan and Chas Shakespeare, Pat Tilley, Phil Waldren, the Hon. Jim Wallace, Margaret Westwood, Sheila Williams, Ray Williams, Halesowen Church School, Halesowen United Church and Stourbridge Library.

BRITAIN IN OLD PHOTOGRAPHS

SUTTON'S PHOTOGRAPHIC HISTORY OF TRANSPORT

To order any of these titles please telephone our distributor, Littlehampton Book Services on 01903 8288
For a catalogue of these and our other titles please ring Emma Leitch on 01453 731114